This book belongs to

....

Thank you to my husband Nesher and sons
Nathan, Owen, and Jacob for allowing me to keep asking,
"So what do you think about this?"
Thank you to Mary Ellen Fricke for her social media help.
Thank you to Karin Blaski for encouraging me
to write and showing it was possible.

Copyright © 2022 Carrie Sharkey Asner
All rights reserved. No parts of this book may be printed, reproduced or utilised in any form by any electronic, mechanical, or any other means, now known or hereafter invented, including photocopying and recording, or in any information or retrieval system, without permission in writing from the publishers.

Illustrations by Marcin Piwowarski
Cover Design by Sean Michael Severino
Format and Layout by Glaiza Beverly Ganaba

Publisher's Cataloging-in-Publication data

Names: Asner, Carrie Sharkey, author. | Piwowarski, Marcin, illustrator.
Title: Blueberry-blue bubble / written by Carrie Sharkey Asner; illustrated by Marcin Piwowarski.
Description: Rockford, IL: Carrie Sharkey Asner, 2022. | Summary: A bubblegum blower blows a blue bubble. But what happens when the bubble gets bigger, and bigger and bigger?
Identifiers: LCCN: 2022914709 | ISBN: ISBN: 978-1-959175-01-8 (hardcover) | 978-1-959175-00-1 (paperback) | 978-1-959175-02-5 (Kindle) | 978-1-959175-03-2 (epub)
Subjects: LCSH Bubble gum--Fiction. | Humorous stories. | BISAC FICTION / Humorous Stories
Classification: LCC PZ7.1 .A86 Bl 2022 | DDC [E]--dc23

Blueberry Blue Bubbles

Carrie Sharkey Asner   Marcin Piwowarski

I take a big breath...

I blow a big bubble.

Watch out, frog!
I blow a bumpy, bendy,
bigger, blueberry-blue bubble.
I want it **bigger!**

Watch out, mouse!
I blow a bouncy, bumpy, bendy,
bigger blueberry-blue bubble.

I want it **bigger!**

Meow!

Watch out, cat!
I blow a balancing,
bouncy, bumpy, bendy,
bigger blueberry-blue bubble.

I want it **bigger!**

Woof!

Watch out, dog!
I blow a beaming, balancing, bouncy, bumpy, bendy, bigger blueberry-blue bubble.

Watch out, cow! Cow?
We don't have a cow!

But, I did spill my milk,
may I have more?

Bye-Bye,
biggest, beaming, balancing, bouncy, bumpy, bendy, bigger blueberry-blue bubble.

Now I want an even bigger piece of gum!

The Author

Carrie Sharkey Asner is a Family Physician who realized the fun of creating children's picture books, and the importance of reading to young children.

The Illustrator

Marcin Piwowarski

 instagram.com/marcin_piwowarski

Visit www.CarrieSharkeyAsner.com for more information and book extras.

CPSIA information can be obtained
at www.ICGtesting.com
Printed in the USA
JSHW062132081122
32871JS00002B/3